David K. Shipler reported for *The New York Times* for over 20 years from New York, Saigon, Moscow, Jerusalem, and Washington, D.C., where he was Chief Diplomatic Correspondent. He is the author of seven previous books, including the bestsellers *Russia* and *The Working Poor*, as well as *Arab and Jew*, which won the Pulitzer Prize. He received a George Polk Award, an Overseas Press Club Award, and, for the PBS documentary *Arab and Jew,* a duPont-Columbia Award for broadcast journalism. He has taught at Dartmouth, Princeton, and American University, and has been a guest scholar at the Brookings Institution, a senior associate at the Carnegie Endowment for International Peace, and a Woodrow Wilson Fellow on more than 25 campuses. He writes online at The Shipler Report and co-hosts the podcast Two Reporters.

The Wind is Invisible

ALSO BY DAVID K. SHIPLER

Freedom of Speech: Mightier Than the Sword

Rights at Risk: The Limits of Liberty in Modern America

The Rights of the People:
How Our Search for Safety Invades Our Liberties

The Working Poor: Invisible in America

A Country of Strangers: Blacks and Whites in America

Arab and Jew: Wounded Spirits in a Promised Land

Russia: Broken Idols, Solemn Dreams

The Wind is Invisible

And Other Poems

David K. Shipler

Stone Lantern Books

First Printing, 2023
Stone Lantern Books
Chevy Chase, MD and Swan's Island, ME

The poem *Varnishing* first appeared in *Island Journal.*

The Library of Congress has catalogued this edition as follows:
Shipler, David K.
The Wind is Invisible: And other poems/David K. Shipler
1. Poetry

Paperback ISBN: 979-8-218-15188-1
eBook ISBN: 979--8-218-15189-8

For Debby

CONTENTS

CONTENTS

WAVELENGTHS

NON-FICTION

OFFSPRING

A Wild Word

I am searching for a word that means everything
or anything, like the wild card in a deck
that liberates the player
Only here, a wild word would liberate
not just the writer, but the reader
into inspiration

AIR

The Wind is Invisible

The wind is invisible
    so does it exist?
The long grasses bend
    to pay the sun homage
The tallest trees fall
    to rest from exhaustion
The ocean turns rough
    to play after calmness
The wind is imagined
    so it cannot be guilty

The wind is a spirit
    teasing the memories
The mourners remember
    what children don't know
The grave is a shelter
    from all the forgetting
The lives leave their traces
    preserved in the spirit
The wind is a spirit
    teasing the memories

The Down of a Thistle

We are floating, drifting, wandering
on lacey parachutes of down
at the whim of unseeable currents
in the warming, in the cooling,
daytime, nighttime, lifting, sinking
colliding, touching, embracing, parting
passing unknown even so close by
at distances unbridgeable
no matter here or far
each seed suspended at the mercy
of its fate to sail and settle
barren in the salty sea
or fruitful in the fertile soil
to bring into next year's moving air
the fleet of chances gained and missed

Ambiguous Days

I dislike ambiguous days
When the sun is bright, but a distant haze
Bodes ill before the light is spent
"Chance of lightning, fifty percent"
In forecasting that's called hedging your bet
And makes me wonder, if the sails are set
The jib sheet's winched, the main is taut
I'm too far from harbor than I ought
And thunder rolls from up the bay
What voice of caution I should obey
To quench the thirst to sail some more
I'll wish I'd simply stayed ashore

I dislike ambiguous days
When the sky is slick with an ominous glaze
And the air's too still, too quiet, too warm
I'd rather have a roaring storm
Than have to guess and squint and ponder
What might be coming from out yonder
Simplicity makes you feel decisive
A fine illusion that you're incisive

Masts

They could be masts against the fog
those two old spruces eastward near
two trunks straight, true
low limbs long gone
now thick black lines drawn on the gray
rising in perfect parallel
anchored by unseen roots below
sustained by needled branches high
top-heavy high
ready to fall in winter's wind

Perhaps when they were saplings slight
great schooners sailed
and shipwrights might have prophesied
summers and winters years from then,
to eye their perfect parallel
for masts straight, true
to sail the winter wind and seas
because in days gone by
life ended in rebirth

As the Storm Dies

In the night the wind rose first
to a low shhhh like the sound of snow
muffling all sharper noises
house sounds, pipe sounds, ticking, chimes.
The wind outside rose then
to the faintest whistle, the prelude to
a scream through branches, the rigging
as if offshore. But no danger here behind
closed doors, snug two-by-sixes
well built enough to go to sea in
windows sealed against the storm
raging comfortably at dawn beyond our risk
ocean wild curling froth angry crashes
on granite so we spectators, merely spectators,
can serve as audience to Poseidon's wrath of
cobalt water an iron liquid fury hurling
itself upon the land, our land. Whose land?

No blood rushes like blood in storms
no more alive than this, like the moment
before perishing in battle, the instant most acute

with all the senses tuned
the storm occupied the morning
slender spruces swayed and whipped as if
to snap like matchsticks
little boats on moorings tossed and ducked
spray rain pelted windows, birdshot
so when at last the gale began to wane
and the seas relaxed their fierce onslaught
and the ting of halyards slapping on the masts
fell silent, trees stood straight, survivors
a surge of sadness at the coming end
the show was over

Holes in the Wind

Even the smoothest sailing
May slacken, slow, and drift,
Held by a hole in the wind,
Invisible, infernal,
A rudder useless,
A course erased,
Amplifying every heaving swell,
Rolling rigging tossed clattering,
Creaking hull sounds unheard before,
Deep turbulence unrestrained.
Doldrums curse adventurers
Who strive and journey within themselves,
And sometimes sail
Through holes in the wind,
From which their strength and patience
Eventually rescue them
With a fair breeze.

The East Wind

The graying wind, the leaden wind
Blows from the solid sea
The island cannot warm this wind
Across to the western lee

The osprey soars in the chilling wind
Floats, dances as at play
Rides innocently the ominous wind
The storm will have its way

No sanctuary from this wind
Bones are not immune
Deep there begins the graying wind
Carving its ancient rune

Waking Up to Fog

Whether fog is cruel or kind
Depends on where you lie
At anchor or at home
In berth or downy bed
To sail or not to try
To sink into the womb
Or navigate the dread

Waking up to fog
Gentles every sound
Suffocates all sight
The pewter water blind
With no reflection found
Depending where you lie
Fog is cruel or kind

LIGHT

Invincible Light

The absence of darkness cannot be vanquished
by any night no matter what its density
for penetrating power resolves to keep
life, promise, all possibility.

Clouds skim, translucent shadows, thin
eyelids cannot close out all colors
water, permeable, allows wavelengths
to twist and slide and infiltrate
to the fears submerged
until they play and dance, make delicate
the hard, the immobile.
Light is indestructible.

First Light

For Ethan

You like to get up early
when the house is quiet.
The day is still clean,
not messy with voices and busy things.
And when you get up early enough,
if you look out of the window
and watch what we call at sea
First Light,
you will be able to take a deep breath
in calm silence
and think for a long moment
about all of your first lights,
how every word that you learn,
every new sentence on a page,
is another light.

Selfies

For Madison

If we all took selfies
And saw ourselves through sweet and sour eyes
Clearly
Neither in rose colors nor in harsh light
But true—well, with slightly softer focus than true
Then we would believe in what we are
And can be
And would not be fooled by silhouettes

Awareness runs at deeper levels than we see
It plays between the shadows and the brightnesses
It surfaces in images and verse
Unconsciously bid, revealing perhaps by accident
Alongside purpose
A riddle for your witnesses
A puzzle disguising something more
Beyond our view

In this way, you are becoming

Becoming what? You may ask
And so you must ask
By wondering at the origins of your poetry and pictures
Without ever quite knowing the answer
Until you hold the camera at arm's length

A Window

Through the window of the moon
A trunk and branches can be viewed
Regard the moment as a boon
To see an earthly landscape skewed
In wild vastness rendered tame
By boundaries of celestial light
Infinity encircled in a frame
Imagine what's beyond our sight

Flat Light

Shadowless snow, shadowless sea,
skiers, sailors cannot know
in the monochrome what undulations
will jostle in their way.
Every mogul, every wave
comes unwarned.

Be prepared. Knees bent, poles ready.
One hand for the boat, one for the rope.
Crouch, stay low.
Take the surprise out of the surprise.
Then, having anticipated the unanticipated,
smile victoriously into the grayness.

Gone

I feel the fog before I see it
A chill shudders in the placid air
The calm before the blindness
All senses tuned acutely
Except for sight
The height of every clarity
Drawn vividly across the rippling water of the cove
Dampness in the bones
Ahead of pain
A gentle coldness
Burrowing quietly
A shiver
Then the far shore of past and future wooded land
Dissolves into gray forgetfulness
Memory dims, vision disappears
Swallowed by the fog
And I am gone

Moon Shadows

If only moon shadows could kiss sun shadows
without being blinded
        into invisibility
The earth could live in dual dimensions
healing itself
        from harshness
while rescuing itself
        from frailty
Just think: warmed and cooled at once
Impelled and soothed
        at once
Venturing out, hibernating
        all at once
Without conflicted restlessness
just yearning
        with contentment

WATER

A Falling Tide

Between Bold and Devil Is.

A falling tide lowers all boats.
In graceful symmetry,
all three of us anchored here
in a bracelet of islands,
sails furled in sheltering twilight,
descend unconsciously
so slowly we cannot tell
that we are falling, falling.

Granite shores glide gently upward.
Gray pink boulders stretch above the edge of
blue pastel.
The glow lasts longest in the water and the sky
against the darkening land, the darkening land,
and now, southeast to seaward,
a spine of smooth stone ledge begins to show,
at first a trace of shadow under water
then a little hump, a tiny peak.
Look away, admire the echoes of the setting sun,

then return your gaze to notice
that the pieces of ledge have been connected
like an ancient backbone now revealed.

You see, these ledges have no secrets.
Unlike their cousins constantly submerged,
this long thin line of rock and barnacles
of tidal pools and green crabs skittering, periwinkles,
rockweed clinging,
of miniature beaches whose sand
is made of shells crushed into as many tiny pieces
as spots of light in the undiscovered universe,
these ledges emerge two times a day.
They hide nothing, nothing
whenever the tide recedes
they are exposed, betrayed.

Now the rocks are black against the lingering blue.
Low tide will come at night
and again in the morning's brightness
when I'll go ashore, explore
the fascinating non-secrets of our falling, falling.
No surprise awaits me
just rediscoveries, always.

Or so I expect.
But when the sun is brilliant
and I pull my dinghy with a hiss on the beach of shells,
I catch lithe movement in the corner of my eye,

and there, gliding among the smooth rocks to my right
a sea mink, slick and slender,
a small green crab between its teeth,
and we, both of us being curious, stop and freeze,
look into each other's eyes
for whatever fragment of time the ebb and flow allows
until the mink breaks off and dodges into
a narrow crevice,
leaving a streak of surprise
on my long history of rediscovery.

Dark Harbour

Here on the flank of Fundy tides
scoured and troubled in the race
inside an oval drawn by stones
from which no outlet can be seen
a placid pond awaits its catch
once lured by fire from nighttime seas
when men hauled driftwood to the height
and struck a match atop that tower
to set a blaze to mesmerize
and bring the herring with the rush
of rising tide through inlet, yes--
it's there, a narrow way pinched tight
a seiner can go through at high

Now netted curves of weathered weirs
ungainly held by crippled poles
hope gracefully against the wrecks
of foregone dreams on ruined shores
the herring come less plentifully
the weathered man with easy smile
explains while waiting for his son

to come with beamy dory here
the father's pulled his pickup down
across the narrow gravel beach
in back two rusty anchors lie
they load the anchors in the boat
"We'll build another weir," says he

Encryption

What script is this
painted on the liquid face
of the tide?
Sheltered, the cove seems tranquil
hidden from the swells outside,
yet surface folds, barely visible,
encode floating images above:
a branch, a bird, a varied light
into a message, bold at first
then trailing off
untranslated

Surface Tension

A brown leaf drifts down, curled and crisp
until it touches the canal
and floats suspended on the surface

A lazy muddy current flows beneath
but against it blows a little breeze
the leaf is caught like a merry sail

Propelled against the deeper current
the leaf defies the gradual gravity of earth
dancing over older leaves grayed and sunken

Where the current imprisons them
and moves them languidly downstream
dead to the frolicking crisp curled leaf above

"Skip a Stone for Me"

For Michael, texting from Kathmandu

I skipped a stone for you
On Butter Island
Chosen from the universe of stones
Worn and polished by the time
That's already run, will run
Beneath the depths
At the sea's edge
Where worlds meet

I found a stone for you
Gray and gently rounded
So smooth it felt soft
So soft my calloused fingers
Didn't want to let it go
From one world to another
And so I held it for a while
On the beach at Butter Island

How would it skip, I wondered

Water is harder than stone
And more patient
Stone is heavier than water
And more stubborn
Would my stone, your stone
Glance lightly off the hard surface
And skip in many brittle jumps?

We always count the skips
And brag the more the better
As if a stone that flits and scatters
Tossed again by every touch of sparkling sea
Plays brilliantly along its path
Fights nobly against its final plunge
When in truth its aimless dance
Makes a superficial journey

We always groan in disappointment
At the stone that merely plops
And disappears without a single hop
So dull and purposeless, a wasted throw
Defensively we blame the stone
Honestly we blame our arm
How would yours skip, I wondered
Into the other world?

It struck the surface of the morning sea
And bounced and sailed
In one long, perfect, graceful arc

As elegant as every rainbow
That has decorated Butter Island
And then plunged cleanly, joyfully
Into the other world
To be polished and smoothed some more

Wind or Tide?

If I watch the wind and not the tide,
There is much the waves and ripples do not say,
I cannot tell which way my boat will ride,
Anchored in a harbor, cove, or bay.

Sometimes the wind plays foolishly against the current deep,
And dances heedlessly to twist my boat awry,
Waves slap the hull and interrupt my sleep,
I cannot tell which way my boat will lie.

When wind and current run in opposition,
All else becomes entirely askew,
The water's face betrays a false condition,
We look beneath to figure what is true.

And what is true, the tide or wind?
In which would I abide,
If the fair breeze sang and the tempest sinned,
Which way would my boat ride?

The winds can frolic and destroy,

But come up fast and disappear,
The solemn tides, in steadfast joy,
Are predicted for a year.

I want my bow and anchor chain,
To line up with the seas,
To weather all the storms and rain,
That defy our panicked pleas.

So contrary winds must die away,
Still the mast against the sky,
Let the deeper current then hold sway,
To tell how my boat will lie.

The Edges of Islands

John Donne was right and wrong
"No man is an island, entire of itself."
Yes, but I am also bound by an island's shores
Though rocky headlands and lacey sands
May beckon to the tempting sea
Though calm blueness grays and gnarls
Exciting yearning wanderlust
The island has an edge

I delight in the edge, the limit, the frontier
Always discoverable by traveling
Far enough in one direction
Until through trees I taste
Mixed into pungent pine tar smells
The whiff of sea, the drink of cooler wind
Plunge onward to the shore and stand
At the edge of myself

Alaska Spring

Winter must have been at silent peace
the tumbling rivers paralyzed
lakes blinding slick unrippled by the wind
cascades sculptured in their fall
before the ice decayed

Land of broad biceps
spine of gold
muscular hillsides hold in check
liquid channels carved in eons
of fathoms unfathomed

Stubborn seeming land, rough resilient land
against the trappers, diggers, drillers, burners
whipping gales below, jagged snow above
stirring now from ice-age
hibernation

The bears are waking up
herring know to spawn
sharp-talon eagles swoop

scoters raft and dive
spouting humpbacks journey to the feast

Between their frozen flanks
rivers cut their fluid paths
cliff-bound waterfalls hung vertically
are now released to plunge
in threaded veils

The face of glacier ice deceptively
invincible is honeycombed
In pastel turquoise crevices
but melted azure pools atop
mean vibrant spring unyielding

Against the white, unblemished white
the startling blue like gems
captivate the eye
"a cancer," says the old Alaska captain
"tumors in the glaciers."

The Following Sea

For Michael

You might think that it's easy
With the wind at your back
But the following sea
Needs your attention
Not a moment to wander in thought
Not an instant to take for granted
The wheel in your hands

If you can dream and exult and concentrate
If you can live beyond the now and in the now
If you can soar freely and intensely
If you can ride the big rollers like flying
And outguess their attempts to throw you off course
If you can do all those things at once laughingly
Your journey will be beautiful

EARTH

Death Grip

The seedling must have fallen
by the low probability
of good fortune
into the slightest crevice of nourishment
where soil windblown across the granite shore
collected, settled, packed itself against
the further squalls and downpours

The seedling must have put out roots
as thin as nerves to touch
the slender line of captured earth
and suck sustenance
seemingly from inside stone
until a hardy sapling stood
supple enough to ride the coastal wind
and keep its footing
sending its grasping roots around the rock
hunting for the nutrients of life

Rising, rising, the tough spruce grew
thickening its grip around the boulder

sturdy in ferocious winter sea storms
until, towering in its age, unsteadily
it could not hold against the gale
and fell in a silent crash
but never loosed its grip upon
the stone, ripped now from the fragile earth

Granite

I used to think of granite
As the hardest thing on earth
(except for diamonds, I knew)
And in my youth
When nothing was vulnerable
Granite stood majestically invincible
Symbolizing permanence

In my middle years
I watched how patiently a stream, a sea
Could wear away the hardest stone
Or, if in a hurry,
Fill the tiny crevices
And wait for winter
So that ice could use its leverage
To crack and split
The hardest thing on earth
(except for diamonds)

In this, my 62nd spring
I set some fires

I burned some brush and timber
On a rocky shore
Amid pink granite ledges
Hard and solid
Deposited by glaciers
Rolled and fashioned by the tides
And the fires, blazing hot
Crackled and hissed
And from time to time
Among the flames and sparks
A rifle shot, and again
A sound as clean as starlight
And when the fire died
And the ashes blew away
The edges of the greatest boulders
Were shattered into flakes of brittle stone
Crumbling in my hands:
The hardest thing on earth.

The Peppermint Spider

So deceptive the bucolic field
Softly peaceful its allure
Disguising all that it may yield
Violence in miniature

For lurking camouflaged in white
On petals of a daisy
Tiny, still, and out of sight
The spider seemed quite lazy

As if in somnolent repose
Waiting for the moment
Frozen in her flowery pose
Poised to loose her torment

Suddenly there fluttered down
A silent moth, oblivious
Alighting now without a sound
Beside the beast carnivorous
The End.

Then came a monstrous bee
Winging blithely to the spider
Which of course it didn't see
Until it was inside her
The End Again.

May

the river is dark
after the rains
carry the earth

Searching for Islands

Searching for islands
You step ashore
And wish, perhaps,
That you could spend
Whatever soothing time
Is needed to explore

Finding islands
Kindles some inner light
Illuminating sand and stone
Bleached shells and bones
That tell an untold mystery
A respite from the flight

Escape to islands
You cannot measure
All jewels buoyant
Glisten on a pulsing sea
That smooths and comforts
And guards their treasure

I Am Killing Wild Roses

Because, you see, they know no moderation
And we middle-ground people like moderation
We resent extremes
As long as the roses thrived only at the edge of the clearing
Where I had no reason to walk
As long as they bloomed prettily, safely at a distance
Where I could admire remotely the diversity of life
As long as they allowed all others to flourish
And posed no threat of domination
I tolerated them, even welcomed them with an open mind

But when a cluster of thorny stems
Appeared close by our dirt road
Then another among the raspberries we like to pick
Then near the bayberries, which had to struggle to survive
First here, then over there
And when the stems rose tall, straight
Startling little spruce saplings
Choking, spreading

You see, some stems were as thick as thumbs
I began to take them seriously
With a blade and a dash of poison

Keeping the Clearing

Out of the dark and tangled wood,
A man straight as iron stepped and stood,
Relieved to breathe before his gaze
The lucid wind across the maze
Of open grasses, tart green in spring,
Swaying liquid poised to sing,
Gliding across relentless reason,
Melodies of the gentle season.

Swinging, swinging the arc of scythe,
Shoulders hunched now twist and writhe,
Fighting for the neglected clearing
Against the spruce and wild rose nearing,
And smothering the old stone wall
Now noticed by the man, once tall,
Who in his yearly chore now bends,
Cutting, cutting as summer ends.

Before, before, long, long before,
Huddled from winter on the shore,
Below unspoiled forest green,

Men sharpened chips of granite keen,
Then later men came, cut, and burned,
Carving out of nature spurned,
This field so open to the sky
That with new life will surely die.

Who will keep the spruce at bay,
The soft-pricked raspberries that give way
To roses' unforgiving thorn,
The graceful grasses bent by scorn?
Who will keep the sunlight keen,
Carpeting the ground with green
When the winter has been done,
And the man is gone?

The History of Picking Raspberries

Skipping quickly past the creation of the universe,
The Big Bang, the fireworks shower of new planets,
Sidestepping God's division into light and darkness,
Then rushing through the age of ice and glaciers
That carved these valleys and those seas
And pushed that granite into hills and islands,
Skimming over all of that, we come to now.

A quick red squirrel forages and saves for deepest winter,
Snaps from high among the branches of a spruce,
A green cone laden with dormant seeds inside,
Then skittering down, across the cooling ground,
Finds a secret hiding place for after hibernation,
But then might not remember before the seeds awaken
As the days get longer seconds at a time.

Tender shoots grow into woods too thick for sunlight,
Spruces struggle upward, lower branches die in shadow,
Winds whip and funnel into hollows, roar up slopes,

Trees crack and crash and tumble, leaving tangled chaos
That takes a decade for tiny beings to devour,
To soften, flake, disintegrate, sink back to the grateful earth,
Warmed again by sunlight from the aging universe.

Grasses grow at first, then low leafed spreading carpets.
Thistles come and go with purple flashes and white down,
And soon the bushes that will finally yield
Reach to the knees, then to the chest, and in July
Decorate the clearing with dots of such a red
That vibrates at the spectrum's place for wine
In sympathetic harmony with deep desire.

I like to use a metal pot so I can hear the clink
As each ripe berry, firm enough to make the sound,
Drops joyously to start the hour's new collection.
Some cry out for picking, trembling obviously in view.
Others are concealed in swaddling thickets.
Lift a leaf, pull aside a stalk.
Avoid if possible the tiny thorns that prick.

If once I make my way through chest-high bushes
And am convinced that every berry's been revealed,
But turn around and venture back the way I've come
To see that suddenly more luscious looking reds appear,
I bend and reach now picking those I missed
Now magically disclosed by angle's shift:
The stunning visibility of history.

Inevitability

In the beginning
spring dusts the brown hills
with the first sour green.
When seen too closely,
tiny leaves drip from skeleton branches
as if on the verge of fluttering down
now, too soon.
Can spring be thwarted?

Before the Snow

Across the lake the leaves are turning, falling
Here on this bank, the last grasses reach and yearn
Before the early darkness settles silently
And makes the earth hard enough for snow

WAVELENGTHS

Goldberg Variations

In Tribute to Glenn Gould

Fingers sheathed in wool
Against the abrasive world
Please do not touch, no shaking
With enemies or friends
Detractors, fans, admirers
These instruments, delicate
Made naked, vulnerable for audiences
Mobs in fur and somber suits
Confused by unfamiliar tempi, clapping meaty hands

Retreat into the sanctuary
Studio. Control.
Tape plays, words and gestures are too slow
The engineer hesitates a beat
Reach over, slide plastic knobs yourself
Each one for a place of listening in the empty hall
Slide this volume up, that volume down, blend the listening
Razor blade on tape, manufacturing perfection
Control.

If only people were like keys
From the very tips of the fingers
Light trickles, pours, punctuating, flowing
Directly from inside the chest just below
The heart.
If only people could be connected
Directly to the vicinity of the heart
So when the brain stops working
Love and music may continue

Music

I am on shore when the wind dies and ceases
to shred and scatter sounds
when fog settles finally in the cove
to justify the ferry's mournful horn
whose song of lamentation ends before it ends
sustained for many seconds in reverberating echo
by the cove's cathedral calm
which holds the single note
as fervently as vaulted arches
keep alive a lingering hymn

An unseen gull cries plaintively
a diesel growls along some distant road
seals grunt out of sight
then, from the far channel, a rhythmic
pure bell toll from the buoy
rocked enough by gentle waves
to tilt clappers into striking cleanly
the first and final haunting notes
of my favorite melody

Dawn

After the clock strikes the hour
The silent beat is louder than the rest
A moment hovering as if to wait
For the punctuating absence
Of the chime that is not there
The sixth if it is five, the seventh if six
Spreading in the darkness
An ink drop sifting through a blotter
Then abandoning its rhythm to a halt

I wake
Time
No pushing back, only gliding forward
Treasure the silent beat
The quiet audience after the last line is spoken
One second, two seconds suspended
After the last note is played
Stretch out the mute reverie
Don't break the spell with accolades
Let the daylight wait

An Instant

It never exists, the motion frozen
The puffin dancing on the surface
Its reflection an abstract splash of ink
The footsteps leaving globules of glass
Suspended without gravity
The sea carved carefully
In velvet contours
These never exist in reality
Only in the artificial instant
Of the camera's imagination

Green Eyes

Speed is the enemy of detail
blurry swiftness mixes colors
smudges lines, makes thoughts flicker
unfocuses the glance
That is the tactic of the darting swallow
the ADHD chipmunk
the drive-by politician
the flitting dragonfly bound to be no one's prey
Stillness is the enemy of shallowness
the medium of contemplation
only when the dragonfly sits frozen for an instant
can you notice its green eyes

Egret on a Branch

As if by some artistic hand
were drawn the graceful swerves
of graying wood and snowy down
the stillness seemed in motion
echoing through every bend and bow
legs and branches intertwined in mood
from somewhere in a common root
a static dance of lines and arcs
where harmonies are soundless

The Chiming of the Clocks

Both clocks have stopped
Silently the house is dead
No sound in the darkness
To ease the dread
As in a tomb impervious
To morning birds' melodic calls
To stars of night and sun of day
To every leaf that greens, then falls
The house is dead
I cannot lie awake, I fear
And count the hourly strokes
Time's run I can no longer hear

NON-FICTION

God is Busy

God is busy
too busy this epoch
to notice us down in Jerusalem
where we think we are closest
to God
in the pastel half light of prayers
in the soft murmurs, pleading
unheard

too busy to come to Kigali
to the churches that run with our blood
too busy to come to Phnom Penh
to our classrooms turned into cells
of torture

too busy for the ravine at Babi Yar,
the gas shower of Auschwitz, the grave of Srebenica,
too busy for our girls of Chibok, Syria, or Chad
for our children of Mariupol and Bucha
of our pious Boston families violated by fathers
and priests

too busy, doing what?
perhaps admiring His creations
entrancing peaks and glaciers, sylvan jungles, deserts
absent the sole creation let loose against
itself

too busy except one time
out of the corner of His eye
noticing a flash over Hiroshima
He blinks but then, too busy, He turns
away

Listen to Us

There would be little bother
And hardly a fuss
If the world would only
Listen to us

If they want to end war
And earn enough pay
And bring up their children
In the very best way
All they must do
Is to do what we say

Whatever the conflict
On land or at sea
We've noticed it's caused
By stupidity
So, for every injustice
Just solve it, say we

Just be nice and perceptive
Be smart and humane

Look to us as the models
It's really quite plain
It's so very easy:
Just try to be sane

We have many years
Of showing the way
Of trying to get them
To do what we say

So in our perfect world
Without bother or fuss
Everybody will simply
Listen to us

Varnishing

Varnishing the truth is a hands-off cliché
Ridden with inexperience
Perhaps by a poet in search of metaphor
Who saw his faint reflection in amber
While gazing at the polished sheen
Of careful wood

For varnishing cannot conceal
Except by long patience
Which I do not have
When varnishing the old mahogany
Or is it teak?
On my boat aged half a century

I cannot spend the tedium
Of sanding all the years of blemishes away
Or stripping, chipping, peeling down the layers
As archeologists dig back in time
Recording hard encounters scarcely noticed
Now decades later, toughened into scars

Old wood is scarred, let's face it
And varnish in the can is liquid pure
Thin, transparent, sealing without hiding
The scrapes and dents and multicolored bruises
Stubborn unless erased, forgotten, submerged by many coats
The truth cannot be varnished

The New Law

Congress outlawed lying
and so then fell silent
leaving the halls echoing
with only the lonely voice
of one who would not be there again
after the people next cast ballots

Truth police roamed the land
listening, watching for mendacity
broadcast, posted, printed, uttered
fear washed columns of type with blank swaths
muzzled the spectrum with dead air and bleeps
TV became commercial-free

History teachers watched their words
award committees granted sparingly
decorations thinned on soldiers' chests
eulogies became the rarity
Beck, O'Reilly shared a cell with Trump
Hannity and Limbaugh walked the prison yard

Certain terms were heard less often:
love, promise, I do, I will
bipartisan, redacted, enhanced interrogation
challenged, developing, extraordinary rendition
gossip disappeared from offices and kitchens
meditation was all the rage

A Cop Cries

A cop cries after shooting to death
an unarmed driver
it's online, the whole world can watch
the video from the dash cam
in blue lights flashing like a disco
the music is weeping, hysterical
the young cop drapes himself across the hood
Billings, Montana Police Department: 04/14/13

"I thought he was gonna pull a gun on me."
sobbing spasms break the young cop open
"Maybe he was. Maybe he was," his colleague says,
the one who puts his arm around his shoulder,
touches his back
in and out of the frame
other cops come and go
staring in wonder, not knowing
how cops are supposed to behave
when one of them is dissolved in weeping
after a killing.

"Come on," says the comforting cop,
"Let's get you out of here."
The weeping music fades away
Blue lights keep flashing, like a disco.
The jury's verdict: not guilty

Errors and Toys

they cannot be casually strewn
across the floor, then
merely swept up in a hand
while the ball is in the air

errors are not jacks
they are never entirely collected
and put away
they have pointed ends

The Math of Cruelty

Take it apart piece by piece,
dismantle mercilessness:
separate necessity from choice,
divide survival from wanton ruthlessness,
calculate the weight of instinct and
the weight of learning,
compute the numerator of trained viciousness,
place it over the denominator of congenital cruelty.

The higher the value,
the closer to humankind.

To rectify the equation,
write the fraction of morality
across the equal sign,
make choice the numerator,
make necessity the denominator.

The smaller the value,
the closer to the infinity of survival
by wild beasts and insects,

the closer to the rationalizations
by humankind.

To balance the terrible heaviness
of learned malice across the equation,
make the numerator of choice larger
and larger until morality
cancels out brutality.

Lobsterboat Names

Kyle Thomas
Criss Tina II
Get It Done
Seanior Moment
Armageddon
Force of Habit
Insanity
Next Week
Defiance
Wildest Dreams
Daily Bread
Enginuity
Final Round
Time Out
Fair Maiden
Buggin' Out
Black Thundah II
Mary Joseph
Hey Cap
Breezy Dawn
Sea Flea

Money Move$
Dream Weaver
Karma
Venom
Lobstah Tales
Still Smokin'
Finest Kind
Somp'n Fishey
↑This End Up
Two of a Kind
Tidewalker
Illusion
Nancy and Jamie
Family Tradition
Sandra David
Never Enough
The Gambler
Lazy Days
Steppin' Up
Kill Switch
No Problem
Dreadnought
Miss Sara
Rough Rider III
Ledgehammer
Thin Line
Centerfold
Wet Dreams
Used and Abused

Long Faces
Orca
Sarah Oakley
Autumn Dawn Faith
Twilight
Freedom

Subject Lines

Congrats
Oh well ...
Fwd: The 23rd Sigh: a post election psalm
The Good News
Votefraud
Draft Documents
Paperless Statements
Missing check?
March Safari
Tanzania
Tet
Fwd: Read, sign and forward on
Classified
Payment Advice Notification
Fwd: Left brain/Right brain
Dallas Faces Race
America's Biggest Threat in 2023
Good News!
Chindo viburnums planted last spring
mixedupjello
Plans and Prompts for Peace Café

The Peer Review

Always the journey is internal
no matter where the external
takes the mind and muscles.
Whatever rigor is required
by hill and mile and quest
for excellence, precision, illumination
of the question without,
the peer review is ultimately within:
at the end of the exploration
that has no end.

A Man

In Cambodia, 1974

The boy in helmet and fatigues
was so short that his rifle
almost dragged along the ground
his webbed belt of grenades and gear
hung crazily and loose
among his larger comrades
trudging toward the sound of gunfire

They were not hurrying
they were not alert with eagerness
and when a stretcher suddenly came the other way
out of the fighting and into the village
with a soldier straining at each end
to carry the soldier lying between them
olive green fatigues smeared red
the boy with the long rifle stopped
and stared
before picking up his heavy steps again
toward the sound of gunfire

Colorless

Pity the person who sees in only black and white
Who misses the startling flash of an idea
Or the gentle hues of gradual discovery
Or the twilight tempering of stark certainty

Pity the certain, the sure, the absolute
The bold dichotomy of light and darkness
The hard edges in place of alluring blurs
Pity those who cannot see colors

Identity

The verb *to be* deceives
I *am* cold. I *am* hungry. I *am* six feet tall.
I *am* eight or eighty.
No.
You *are* more than a temperature
More than an interval between meals
More than a measurement in height or years.
The verb *to be* deceives.

You *are* not always cold.
You feel cold now, that *is* not your essence.
You *are* not always hungry.
You feel hungry now, that *is* not your being.
You have not always *been* six feet tall.
You *are* not always eight, or eighty.
Those *are* not who you *are*.

You *are* what cannot be felt or measured
You *are* what you carry with you always
You *are* incalculable, beyond adjectives
Beyond the verb *to be*.

Patriotic Predator

Pride and noble beauty can't disguise
Ferocity embedded in the piercing gaze
Determined danger in the sickle curve of beak
The deadly points of bill and talon spikes
Like lethal arguments immune from all retorts
The vulnerable cannot reason with the eagle

Regal worthiness and raptor's cruelty
Which is true between the dueling pair?
No evil done in such a glorious cloak
Can be as shamed as done in ugliness
Yet splendor puts an edge on killing, greed, and theft
So both are true between the dueling pair

Float majestically on straight-edged wings
Pose as if above the wind to see
Who will look on high admiringly
The brave or innocent revere
While prey know instinctively to dart
Away, away into secure oblivion

Primal Scream

The threat is not always in the frame
nor has it descended yet to seize
with daring and ferocity
the warmed future in the rocky nest
defended only by the scream of rage
the final weapon in the arsenal
of panic as the penguin parent
holds off the swooping skua
at the junction of life and death
in the mild Antarctic summer

Which Side is Up?

"I once wondered," the toucan said,
"why every bird would always perch
with funny feet below its head
so that it could not ever search
for fruit down on a slender branch
too delicate for heavy me
and therefore never have the chance
for yummy treats low on this tree."

The macaw with plumes fiery red
just heard the toucan wondering
so landed screeching with its head
above its feet, then blundering,
turned upside down to reach with greed
a juicy something it could tell
would be delicious—without heed
it grasped, then slipped, and then it fell

The dazed macaw was mighty sore
The toucan wondered never more

TRACES

Traces

For Laura

Traces you leave
across the surfaces of lives
are mere suggestions
of deeper marks,
how permanent you cannot know.

Corners you turn
when only passing through
with companions briefly by the hand,
just meandering, perhaps, or
firmly settling on a path.

Melodies you hum
sing and disappear,
but maybe they register
on someone's inner ear
as harmonies in a core.

You may wonder
what you leave behind,

doubting it's at all profound.
Is it changed from what you find?
I think so.

Walking the Vanished Road

At long last the woods have taken charge
And buried under ages of decay
The ruts once traveled on this way
By those long gone before

Made unseen by fallen leaves
Except for a slight indented parallel
Reminders that the tales we tell
Leave traces to recall

Between low tired walls of stones
Once lifted out to clear some bygone fields
And run in rows like hapless shields
Against contesting lands

A scampering child through dappled shade
With fishing pole instead of books
A can of worms, a box of hooks
Off to sit and watch the pond a while

A couple bent and slow

The road a gentle memory to see
A way to nowhere you could flee
Meander into thoughts

On this road you'd have learned imagining
A forest gremlin, ghosts, an elf
Adventures from inside yourself
To fill the silence of the woods

You'd have wondered then who built this road
And still don't know
For nowhere does it go
But fades and finally disappears

Finding a Beach in Winter

If you want to make a mark,
walk where none has gone before,
find a beach in winter
where no traces have been left
since the last high tide,
sliding back and forth in curves of foam,
has smoothed the sand,
or since the last wind,
blowing with persistent gentleness, with sudden force,
has recarved the stretch of solitude,
into scalloped ripples like an aged shell,
bounded by sea and dunes—
and by the distant point.

If you want to see your mark,
turn at the distant point,
retrace the trace,
that you have drawn through smoothed aloneness,
and follow the sketchy way
that ambles at the edge of curving foam,
here, erased by a playful sea,

there, shuffling up to the looming dunes,
and back along the broad emptiness again.

"Ah, here is where I sat and meditated on the sea.
Here is where my risky step was punished by a wetting.
Here may be where I stooped
to choose the shard of sea-green glass
I finger in my pocket,
worn so it deceives in feeling soft.
Here I ran and nearly tripped,
then, chastened, moved in measured strides,
straight and true,
as if I knew my destination."

Be sure to turn
and retrace your trace,
in time that you can see where you began,
before the light fades at sunset.

Perhaps We'll Hear an Owl

The present is too beautiful
to last
The golden hour before dusk
feels fleeting
It's fading as I write
this verse
The gulls' cries will be carried
away in the evening wind
The water's vibrant blue
will flatten
The granite's glow in the final light
will darken into black
Black against the lingering
sea color

But then, just now, an eagle comes
floating in the evening wind
The water takes the pink reflection
of the western sky
A seal growls from toward
the ledge

Black shore boulders gradually
turn velvet
Wind gentles in the night
to silent softness
The sky will soon sparkle when
Jupiter is up
Perhaps we'll hear an owl
once again

The present is too beautiful to last
But every moment is the present

Innocent Eyes

For Sweta

Somewhere I imagine a child
whose innocent eyes
have lost their innocence,
whose fragile growing
has been stunted,
whose family of others
is afflicted with absences,
whose imagination
has been bruised and wounded,
whose dreams
have dimmed and darkened

And whose future
has now been touched
by a measure of your grace
impossible to measure,
crucial in some incalculable way
in altering some unpredictable fate,
transforming something invisibly

so that maybe, just perhaps,
her child will have innocent eyes.

I Marked a Path

I marked a path
To take us through the tangled spruce
Along the granite shore
Off our well-worn ways
Where we have gone before

Rough coils of pot warp in my hand
Salt-soaked, discarded from their use
I cut lengths and tied them round some trees
To sketch a route
That we might walk with ease

But soon the granite rose
Curved sheer along the cove
And inland, on flat ground
The notion of a straight, smooth trail
Was lost in snarled trees the winters had blown down

It would be nice, I thought
To let ourselves just rove
Within the solitude that we hold dear

But the woods are thick, the ledges steep
Perhaps we'll cut the path next year

Time

Time is to be celebrated,
Lamented, wasted, used,
Respected, spent, and honored.
It passes, runs, goes by, will tell,
Flies, drags, erodes, and heals,
Mellows and enriches.

Time is a tincture,
Indelibly etching stone.
Only looking back across the span
Can you read engravings
On lives you've marked
In pursuit of happiness.

LOVE

The Chance of Meeting

How miniscule a deviation
would set the machinery of fate
awry
How finely tooled, how minute the tolerance,
how vulnerable our happiness
to a moment misaligned
The perfection of coincidence
meshes gingerly
in every moving part
poised to quiver
if an impish flaw
steals opportunity

Permanence

(Tide and a Heart)

How futile it seems to draw and write
between the high and the low tide marks
in malleable sand of soft forgetfulness
when the tide comes and smooths, erases,
leaves behind no clue for others to guess
at the memories as permanent
as if they had been chiseled into stone.

Home

Home.
I like the crowded alleys of the Old City
And the tense camps of the West Bank
And the schools and villages of other languages
Only because of you.
I have liked the roaming and asking
The exploring and listening
In the streets of Saigon and the kitchens of Moscow
The tenements of New York and the embassies of Washington
Among the addicts and professors
The destitute and famous
Only because I can then tell you.
For me all super highways and all dirt pathways
Lead home.

Dimensions

Against the silver-plated fog,
Against the sky-blank final light
Mirrored dusk on water,
Framed in dawns and sunsets,
Encircled by a beaming moon,
Black branches, dark leaves
Flat brooding boulders.
A cardboard cutout couple holding hands
Leave the third dimension for the eye to fill
By carrying from what is known
Of depth and color
Into the silhouettes

Surprise Party

A surprise is a lie of silences,
webs woven of words,
finally torn delightfully by truth,
flung back by good deeds,
reflecting not the common truths
of harsh or sad or glaring,
but a truth repaying all the happiness,
dispensed to distant reaches,
from your great reservoir of caring

Alone on the Boat

Alone on the boat
I feel you there
and carefully don't bump
as I get up
and gingerly avoid
your "blue shoes"
as if they were where I step
in the night.

In my head I talk to you,
share the rising moon with you,
the setting sun,
watch the osprey with a fish,
the blubbery seals wriggle off a ledge,
the kingfisher dart,
all with you.
I always feel you there.

The Line of Solitude

Some years ago I walked a beach,
I can't remember where,
Roque Island, Butter, Orono perhaps,
I do recall you were not there.
Yet I was not alone.

Wistful in your absence,
Where water meets the land,
I watched the slender line,
Move up and down the sand,
Too gently for the missing.

So is solitude a curve
Of sad simplicity,
A graceful edge, a joining,
That needs both land and sea,
As my solitudes need you.

When I walk a beach, I want the sea.
From sea, I want the shore
The lines of solitudes embrace

The longings we explore
Between the self and us.

On a Mother's Death

You fill the hollows of our sounds,
And soothe the longing for the song,
You smooth the yearning for the cadence
Of a mother's lullaby.
You mull the mellow reminiscences,
And color restless seas and sunsets,
You cup your concave hand in mine,
And bring the circle round.
You hear the melodies unsung,
And listen gently to the silence,
You know the rhythms we don't hear,
In the deepest wells of wanting.

To Feel the Waning Wind

Singularity runs at ocean's brink
The clean thin line of tides
Falling up and back across the sand
The pulse of breath that glides
Falling up and back across the sand

Aloneness stands at the island's edge
On a sliver of crescent moon
So simple in the rainless day
Etched in the dusky gloom
So simple in the rainless day

Yet singularity is incomplete
Bare beauty brings a melancholy view
To hear the gulls and feel the waning wind
I need not solitude, but you
To hear the gulls and feel the waning wind

Some Mystery

It was not quite autumn then,
The end of summer blushed and sparkled,
The lantern stood in quiet.
Marking a spot for us,
The seclusion of our comfort,
In which we still find solace,
In all the rush of seasons past and coming.

So tender then, so warm.
How can it have become more tender still?
How can warmth have deepened so?
How can our moments have grown more precious?
Than on that crystal day so long ago?

Some mystery, love.
It rides the rush of seasons,
It moves beneath the earth,
It weds, one to another.

Silences

Then your cup runneth over
and the brook laughs sliding
over discords submerged
blurred slippery smooth
blithely forgotten

Then a torrent of drought
strains the brook down
showing rock-craggy
friction resurfaced
draining the eddies

Then your cup runneth over . . .

OFFSPRING

When the Late Light Dances

For Laura

This is the season when the late light dances
In long and slanting statements of enchantment
In lively cold, the leaves translucent
Quietly drifting through their final chances

They say that autumn is the ending
Of the summer sweetness languishing
That now the days have no more mingling
The air turns brittle, the breath unbending

But only on the surface of the earth
Where wind and sun and temperature are felt
Down deep, things cannot freeze or melt
(The elves reign there in merry mirth!)

Into this season you arrived
With wind and sun and dancing light
To reach for life with all your might
So roots of steadiness have thrived

How luckily you occupy
Both surface fun and insights deep
Where moral values never sleep
And wit and humor taste so wry

My fondest recollections swarm
Where you came home in the autumn glow
The days were long, the nights were slow
And you kept our winter warm

Newborn

For Sweta

When she looks into your face,
Dark eyes unwavering,
And little breezes of contentment
Blow curls of smiles to her lips,
And you bend toward her
In that ancient arc of motherhood,
One pull confronts the other
At the universal junction
Where the tugs and choices
Push between work and home,
The swirling cross-currents
Are the woman's burden,
Laden by the liberation,
That now confronts you
With two joys.

In the Newest Eyes

Reflections in mirrors are precise
in windows, double images
on still waters, trembling
along fluid ripples
deeper than real
through camera lenses, framed and focused
paused, suspended

And in the newest eyes
wide with wonder
at your rhymes and smiles
the gift of fresh devotion
cascades from reflections past
into a present of perfect truth

A Seedling

For Glynis

At the edge of a clearing
where the woods begin (or end)
a tiny spruce pokes tentatively
through the long and bending grass
under the outer reach of a graceful arm
of the towering tree beside.

How can the tree protect the seedling?
For now, it blocks the wind
and anyway, the little one is supple
anchored in the soil held firm
by the big tree's spreading roots
nourished by the needles
falling in a fertile carpet.

I think if the tree
could grasp the seedling as it grows,
could hold it upright in the sun
against the storms,

could flick away
the devastating beetles
and make the right amount of rain,
it would be done
as you are doing.

Of course, the seedling will get tall enough
to face the wind.

Who is the Littler Boy?

For Matt

I cannot tell
Who is the littler boy
Who has the greater glee
The purer feelings
Coursing more completely
Through every cell and synapse
Whose face crinkles more with smiles
Or more with consternation
Whose eyes lock on more lovingly
Whose cooing comes from a deeper well
Of contentment more abiding
Of devotion more impassioned
I cannot tell
Who is the littler boy
Until one changes
The other's diaper

Lap Child

For Jonny

No tender instant
dilutes the strife
of our small planet's
unruly life
more reassuringly
than children
on their father's lap

No laptop hugs
quiet the fear
of whatever worries
might be near
more softly, warmly
than seeing your arms
around your children.

The Lilt

Some of the most beautiful music in the world
Is the lilt in a father's voice,
Following the upward curve
Of talent, of hurdles crossed,
Into a melody of happiness
That rings, clear and strong,
Like a church bell on a snowy night

Heartbeat to Heartbeat

Now you know how it feels
To be a safe and comforting place
To soothe as you were soothed
Into the harmony of sleep
Exchanging warmth, chest to chest
Heartbeat to heartbeat
Tiny Kalpana melting into you
Binding and freeing in ways yet unseen
Drawing you into her dawn,
Your dawn
Where it's scary
To be so reassuring

Wonder

For Laura

I first saw wonder
through your eyes
as if I had never noticed
the sunlight dancing

I first saw smiles
and heard laughter
as if I had never realized
the power of joy

I learned to listen
to your questions
as if I had never taken in
the meaning of "why"

I first watched fantasy
play on your stage
as if I had never known
imagination

I journeyed distances
through your explorations
as if I had never traveled
with an open gaze

I felt the troubles
of your larger world
as if I had never thought
about danger

And now I see
the wonder in your eyes
as if I had never seen before
the sunlight dance of motherhood

An Impish Smile

When Dylan tells a story
How can I tell if it's true?
Even if scary and gory
Is there a little clue?

I'm looking at his eyes
To see if they are clear
Expecting some surprise
Perhaps a little tear

But no, a sparkle's always there
And so I look to see
If something in his hair
Will give a hint to me

Aha! His lips look tight
As if he's really trying
With all his boyish might
To mask his playful lying

For there, just right behind

Dancing all the while
Look closely, you will find
A fetching, impish smile

Word Castles

For Priya, 4

She tumbles over words
And words spill over her
She tosses and bounces them
She juggles them and
Strings them into necklaces
She lines them up and piles them
On top of thoughts and wants
She scatters them across the room
Then picks them up
And puts them in her pockets

She makes towers from her words
And castles
She scares away the monsters with her words
And ghosts
She listens closely to her words
To see what they are saying
And sings them in her head
Where at night when she's in bed
They finally go to sleep

Why?

For Kalpana, 3

Whose favorite word is always "why?"
Who says it when she wants to try
to get grownups please to explain
why this, why that, why everything?

I know that she will want to know
what makes the rain, what makes the snow,
why are bamboo leaves so, so green,
why do you have to wear sunscreen?

Why, oh why, is pastrami red?
Why is it time to go to bed
when there are questions still to ask,
and it's not dark outside, alas?

I'm getting set for all these why's,
so in the night and come sunrise
I'll think and think and make my brain
work very hard to best explain

how this old world goes round and round,
what keeps a butterfly off the ground,
and why call it a butterfly?
Is it made of butter? Oh, my, I'll try

to get the information right,
to satisfy those eyes so bright,
and yet I'll sure be baffled, so
I'll have to say, I just don't know.

And then I'll have to just find out
and learn what everything's about,
so thanks for giving me that task,
and knowing what fun it is to ask!

We Must Be Alike

For Kalpana, 4

What do you like?
Do you like to smile?
Yes. So do I.
Do you like to laugh?
Yes. Me, too.
Do you like to make other people laugh?
You sure do. I do too.
We must be a lot alike.

Do you like steak?
Yes. Me, too. Yum.
Do you like to run around in circles
behind something where you can't be seen
and then come out laughing?
Yes. Me, too, but I can't laugh quite as merrily
as a tumbling brook and a dancing breeze.

Do you like to play hide and seek?
Yes. Me, too.

Do you like to pick blueberries,
look closely at flowers,
hold snowflakes in your hand,
build blocks in towers to the sky?
Yes. So do I.
But mostly I like to watch you doing what you like.

Do you like to draw letters, read words,
color with crayons,
figure out wonderful games,
and stretch out bedtime with a pretend nap
which means "activities"
and many songs and a monster dance?
And questions?
Yes. And even though it goes on and on
I like that you like to do all that.
So we must be very much alike

Are you smart?
Yes. Me, too.
See? We're very much alike.

Bees

For Ethan, 3

Ball, Bat, Boy,
The Boy Bats the Ball Boldly,
Beaming Brilliantly,
Babbling, Bubbling,
Because Balls are Better than Balloons,
Which Bounce Boundlessly Beyond,
But Burst Badly,
Like Bath Bubbles,
So Beware of Bamboozling Balloons,
Which go Bang!

Stretching Your Arms

For Ethan

Stretching your arms
until your hands are in front
of the shooter's eyes
so he cannot focus on the basket

Stretching your long legs
until your arms are so close
to the quarterback
that he cannot find a passing lane

Stretching your mind
gradually upward
like your arms and hands
but not to block--to reach

If I Were a Book

For Kalpana

If I were a book you would read me
And I would open a window
Pull aside a curtain
Let light into your imagination
Take you into other people's thoughts
Carry you far into distant places
Show you beauty and some troubles, too
And give you the gift of being
Even more than who you are so far
Page after page after page

If you were a book I would read you
And you would share your merry laughter
Tell me your questions
Ask me to think and think
Take me far into your games and playing
Show me goodness and worry

Teach me to see the world anew
And give me the gift of being
Even more than who I am so far
Page after page after page

How Boring!

For Ben

Imagine if you knew which way
the ball would bounce
and how its spin
would satisfy your goal
Imagine if you knew just so
undoubtedly, infallibly
without a guess or wonder
the course of every kick
Imagine if you always knew
how you'd do in every class
which friends you'd make
what every day would bring
Imagine if you knew for sure
what haircut you would have next year
what journeys on your own you'd take
how far your limits would extend
Imagine how boring that would be
with pure predictability
a game, a life with certainty
surely not your cup of tea!

Mount Kilimanjaro

For Matt

I think you climb
because you need to gaze,
beyond and close at hand,
to see as far
as imagination can embrace,
to see as near
as compassion cares.

I'll bet from the mountain top,
you can contemplate
the tiny stone lying at your feet,
and feel the instant of the moment
in the wind,
and still look across the ancient hills and plains,
into the throbbing time.

You struggle to the summit,
through cold and thinning air,
to gain the view

that propels all that you do,
to cure the tiny at the moment
by harnessing the long,
large, broad, and far.

The Place of Sloping Granite

For Laura

How were we to know
That the path we cut
Would lead to a special place:
That sloping granite ledge
Adorned with webs of lichen
A respite from the tangled woods
Waiting in surprise
To be come upon without design
A sheltered opening, a graceful inclination
To rest protected yet aloft
Watching the bedrock
Fall gradually away
To sea shimmering through spruces

Finding a place that has been found
Yet needs more finding
Searching for what has been discovered
Yet needs more searching
Yearning for harmony that sounds its chords

Yet needs the dissonance of fervor
To transform the larger landscape
And so enlarge your special place
Which you are seeking
Which you are finding

Welcome to the Teens

For Madison

Welcome to the teens
I remember them well
so let me give you just a glimpse
of what your world will be

Your parents will become
The smartest people on the earth
Not the least embarrassing
and everything they say
you'll think, hmm, that makes sense

Your brother will become
So kind and generous a soul
he'll share with such abandon
you'll think, hmm, how come we never argue?

Your grandfathers will be infinitely wise
You'll sit at their feet entranced
your grandmothers will be always right

wellsprings of sound advice

Your teachers, ever brilliant
Will impart the deepest truths
Hear your excellent analysis in class
and perceive with great appreciation
your remarkable intelligence

Your friends will always be your friends
Loyalty will never be assailed
no gossip, cliques, or meanness
will undermine affection and regard

Those are my wishes
Welcome to the teens

Of Choosing and of Chance

For Madison

Imagine if it were as clear as Robert Frost described
Two roads diverging, one less traveled by
To know how "way leads on to way"
And what lies out of sight beyond the curve and hill
Before we step ahead and choose our path

Suppose we pick the road, as Frost lay claim to doing
Instead of mixing choice with being chosen
At real-life junctions of choosing and of chance
And through clairvoyance see the future landscape
Carved in contours by decisions in the now

It would be an arid place, no pools of mystery
Would sparkle in discovery, no bending doubt
Would make our eyes adjust to shadows
Wanting and selecting would collapse together
Into easy comfort too soothing for the striving heart

Comfort zones are meant to be defied

Resisted, breached, abandoned, left behind
For friction creates traction, and hard ground
Needs gripping for a journey to be made
Along a road of chance and choosing

Biking

Every mile is a world
when your eyes are open.
Every chance encounter is a story
when you listen.
Every life's a universe
when you're curious and care.
Enjoy this stretch of road
and you'll celebrate the next,
around the curve, beyond the hill,
a village unfathomed, a field unplowed,
where every small connection,
and every mile, is a world,
because your eyes are open.

The Only Peace

For Michael

Every journey is a verse,
Fashioned from a dream,
Not fully seen until it's done,
A moment after waking.

Every routing is a line,
Connecting thought and word,
Translated into hope and tune,
Offered for the taking.

Every mile is a note,
In rhythms of designs,
Played into songs of anxious joy:
A life is in the making.

Every journey is a poem,
A yearning search alone,
The only peace the traveler has,
Is the moment after waking.

AGE

October Secrets

We are the last of the summer people,
now become the autumn people,
finally privy to the secrets
annually hidden from the departed
who never see the ferns turn golden,
the crimson carpets of blueberry leaves,
the splashes of yellow birches
hiding within the never-ending green
of living spruces that always outnumber
the dying.

Those who flee before the crystal nights,
before the reborn days of vivid winds,
miss the taste of newness in the skies,
the icy clarity of long infinity
across the cove whose shore seems distant now,
the water startling blue,
the islands poised in layers endlessly beyond,
waiting, waiting for winter.
We shall flee as well before
and miss the secrets of December.

I Have the Habit of a Limp

I have the habit of a limp
though the ankle bone's long healed
and the "soft tissue" too, the doctor says
but still I walk unevenly
a hesitation in my gait
as if afraid of falling
into an old and hidden wound

I cannot find the pain
which leaves alone the burning
its ache is somewhere distant from the bone
diffuse, a blur of memory
I wobble on my feet
does anybody notice
I have the habit of a limp?

Hobbies Found and Lost

By the mere chance of inconvenience
the music stand is put away against
the wall that bears chart 13325,
so that Mozart's Duet No. 1 for Violin and Viola
runs seaward from Mistake Island
onto the Atlantic to the east
covering the deepest soundings with
the most brilliant notes.

The marks on paper look permanent,
as perpetual depths of sea and music,
but grow unusable because
of faltering steps and stiffened hands.
How can what's lost revive
as a crescendo of windswept harmonies?

The charts and scores cannot survive
in a universe of human negligence
without the vision and creative ear
to save the sea from rising
to save the notes from fading.

As soundings, flooded, and sounds, forgotten
pass into ancient maps and manuscripts
how can what's extinct revive
despite our faltering steps and stiffened hands
as a crescendo of windswept harmonies?

Whatever Distance

However the arithmetic adds up
or subtracts to leave whatever distance
is yet to go,
numbers, mere numbers cannot measure
the expanding landscape
of our journeys through devotion

If I could write it down
and plan it out in retrospect,
I would have it exactly as it was,
every climb and turn and mile,
all the potholes and smoothnesses,
the close fogs and the clarity,
the cascade of years gone and coming
as we race a bit against ourselves,
hurrying to reach and grab and hold
as long as we are able

Terror

There is nothing wrong that I know
and so I must stop waiting
for the bomb ticking somewhere
to find a particular failure
in some cell or valve or vital part
now working perfectly, it seems
then someday, here inside
or inside those I love
ripping through the present sweetness
tearing the gliding pleasure
of my final decades.
I must stop waiting

When If

When if became the pivot of the plans
When when became a shell of flesh and bone
A future meant a fragile way of sands
To try to tread uncertainly alone

If when was once the solid ground I knew
I can no longer feel beneath my feet
My course will finally falter and then slew
No matter how monotonous the beat

To look ahead look back before the if
Remember how the firm step landed then
Recall the inner compass course so stiff
To gain again the time when if was when

Soul and Body

They say that the soul leaves the body
and weaves a vapor into the beyond
But I see instead that the body
leaves the soul
which stays, an inner force
Luminous within the grayness
Vibrant beneath the thinning flesh
Steadfast against the sagging skin
Restless in the cage of bones

No, the soul is telling us
as we watch slip away
what we can touch
Not to overlook
what we cannot touch
what cannot be lost
to the betrayal of decay
But remains behind
When all else departs

POEMS TO MYSELF

Priorities

I have chores to do this morning
So I am walking in the woods

I have chores to do this evening
So I am watching the twilight

I have writing to do
So I am reading poetry

I have thinking to do
So I am listening to music

It is Not the Night I Fear

It is not the night I fear
But dusk as it draws near
Misshapen shadows dance
Play their game of chance
The odds are always slim
Dancing on fate's rim

It is not the night I fear
Deep sleep can never hear
But consciousness goes reeling
Blurry, dizzy, kneeling
Half light, I still can see
Where I want to be

Pain is a Liquid

It evaporates after it is gone
impossible to recall
precisely enough to map
a flowing toxic course
impossible to paint
in red that burns enough
or blue that aches enough
impossible, impossible to hear

Only in the moment when it screams
the currents cross and undulate
hot backwater steaming rage
howls in the night, the night
no escape from infiltration
gravity reverses so the flood
passes upward, upward from the source
into suffocated sounds

Failure

is a thin high note
sustained infinitely straight
as a gossamer steel thread
piercing indefinite space
unseen except in certain darkness
unheard except in certain silence
tangling with other failures
in blinding cacophony

Hope

Hope would be translucent if the light
were glowing through the paper wings
of possibility

Hope would be buoyant if we
could catch it in flight and hold it
before it sails away

Hope would be protected if we
cupped it delicately in our hands
without brushing the wings

Round the Next of Kin

Round the next of kin
the ocean bends
to the winter's hard contour
It's the journey's sin
if the voyage ends
in a course as yet unsure

Without the fear
of a tack that's wrong
by sextant and the sun
Sail through the year
sing a yearning song
as on a tossing run

May our hearts be deep
in our others' cause
for devotion we shall strive
So we do not sleep
and we never pause
to keep our souls alive

Fog

Quiet is my cove,
Soft is the mossy bank,
Shaded by birch and spruce.

Gentle is the breeze,
Though far out across the water,
Scudding clouds of ripples
Hint at the sea wind beyond
That now begins to push
The smoke of ocean fog
Across the island,
Tripping over hills,
Sifting through the tallest trees.

I know what it is like out there,
Fierce and dangerous,
But I don't care.
My cove is quiet.

Two Hands

One is cold, one is hot
So if I clasp them together on my lap
While listening to an orchestra play Beethoven
The cold hand chills the warm uncomfortably

And if I lay them across each other on my chest
While I try to sleep
Thinking about them as I doze
The hot hand heats the cold unbearably

The left might be cold, the right hot
Or vice versa
So the man who shakes hands with me
Never knows me thoroughly

Knows me only as cold or
Overwrought
When neither is the case
Which hand shall I play?

Thank You for My Service

The familiar sentence of gratitude,
tossed toward others deserving,
came to me like a gently looping ball,
arcing easily enough for catching.
"Thank you for your service,"
the college president declared,
glancing my way from the lectern.

Not out of knowing that my service,
distilled in a brief phrase in my bio,
handed her just before my time to speak,
was given during utter peace at sea,
while comrades fought and bled in jungles,
she gave a nod to my shabby naval résumé,
to my two years exulting on the ocean.

Through long balmy days and crystal nights,
in storms of terrible beauty and wonderful rage,
embraced by cobalt blue and Homer's wine-dark mystery,
in ports of narrow alleyways and tempting chants,
of siren songs to wandering and seeking,

this intoxicated voyager committed no service,
but was served, was served, the résumé conceals.

She did not know. I knew that there,
in the front row, the strapping man,
his cane propped against his knee,
had brought back wounds and memories,
twice in Iraq, once Afghanistan,
proudly never lost a man, just nearly himself.
I did not catch the gently looping ball.
I left it for him.

Sad-Eyed Seal

Basking on the granite ledge
Blubbery in the summer sun
Then undulating to the edge
You sure look like you weigh a ton

But in the water deep and cold
Where fish abundant can be had
You're lithe and graceful, so I'm told
Why do you always look so sad?

A Puzzling Paradox

Gaps and spaces
open up
in times and places
planned and helpless
small sequesters
sweeping vistas
perhaps to fill
or leave alone
turbulent or still

Free, restrained:
a puzzling paradox
liberated, pained
boundaries now invisible
so more elusive
to sheer willfulness

For what you cannot see
you cannot conquer
to know what you will be

Lanterns

The glow of blurry recollections
float among the clanging church bells
above the snapping firecrackers
now beyond reach
on a course not planned
nudged by a high breeze
unfelt on the humid streets
of Reconquista.

I have never before been to Reconquista
on Christmas Eve at midnight
when the feasting is done and the church bells chime
and eager hands in the squares cradle gently
the fragile paper lanterns
lighting the candles within
careful not to burn the memories
then setting them free to rise, rise
above the roofs and spires
into a misty distance.

I have never before been to Reconquista

or seen the lanterns
but I remember them.
They remind me of my mother.
She would have loved the bells and lanterns
of Reconquista.

The End of Christmas

What if this fragile ball of colored glass
Were the last decoration
Rescued from my mother's basement
Selected for keeping amid the tears
And fit as gently as a blown and painted eggshell
Into the old carton's square compartment?

What if all the others, carefully chosen:
The red one frosted with snowflakes
The one of translucent blue tied with threadbare ribbon
The glass angel, silvery and gold,
What if they had all broken, one every year or so
Falling from the dry and sagging branches
Knocked by a dog's tail, a child's playfulness
Dropped in a moment's inattention
Leaving only this final dingy sphere
Whose gloss once caught merriment in miniature?

What if my hand trembles
As I reach to take it off the tree
And suffocate beneath the memory

Of solitary weeping in my mother's basement
When I found the decorations and had to learn
The sweeter the memory, the sharper the pain
The edge of fondness cuts cold
And makes warm wounds
That ache beautifully?
What if my hand trembles?

But it is not the last decoration,
Not yet.

AUTHOR'S NOTE

The poems in the section called "Love" were inspired by my wife, Debby, whose lifelong companionship has stirred my need to write verses as a way of capturing, somehow, the ecstasy and wonder of the natural world, the thrill of being on or by the sea, the joys of close family, the comedy of life, and the fear of aging. She has opened my heart to whatever poetry dwells within.

The poems in the section entitled "Offspring," and some scattered elsewhere in this collection, were originally written for family on various occasions. It is a tradition, following one established by Debby's father, Harold Isaacs, to present a poem on every birthday, every graduation, every wedding. I have happily kept the ritual alive. Those included here I chose for their universal chords, which reverberate beyond our circle. Some are dedicated by name: Jonny, Laura, and Michael are my children. Glynis, Matt, and Sweta are their spouses. Madison, Ethan, Ben, Kalpana, Dylan, and Priya are my grandchildren. They are all responsible for nurturing the muse.

D.K.S.

Milton Keynes UK
Ingram Content Group UK Ltd.
UKHW011035201123
432908UK00005BA/740